Exciting Writing

A Handbook For Kids

by Lisa Funari Willever

To The New Canaan Library
Enjoy!!
Lisa Funari Willever
2005

Franklin Mason Press

For every kid, everywhere,
because you all have a story to tell....LFW

Franklin Mason Press ISBN 0-9760469-1-1
Library of Congress Control Number 2004112744

Text Copyright © 2004 Lisa Funari Willever
Cover Design by Peri Poloni www.knockoutbooks.com

Editorial Staff: Marcia Jacobs, Brooks Spencer, Linda Funari

www.franklinmasonpress.com

Table of Contents

From The Desk of Lisa Funari Willever

Hello! My name is Lisa Funari Willever and I am so happy to be able to write a book about writing for kids. As an author and a former teacher (that's right, a former teacher), my goal is to make kids excited about writing.

Before I talk about writing, though, I should tell you a little bit about myself. My writing career started many years ago, when I was about eight years old. Without revealing how old I am, I can tell you that this was before people had computer's in their houses. Believe it or not, no one ever thought about having a computer since computers used to be bigger than refrigerators.

My first stories were written in an old spiral notebook. I usually wrote about things I enjoyed and always used my family and friends as the main characters. Of course, because I was the author, I was always the heroine!

Later, that year, my grandmother fixed up her back bedroom, complete with a desk and one of the fanciest things I had ever seen...an electric typewriter.

Well, I took one look at that typewriter and I fell in love. I would beg to sleep over just so I could type stories. Every time I earned some money, I bought typing paper. That's how my love of writing was born and I decided to one day become an author.

I wish that I could tell you I went from writing in my grandmother's back bedroom right to publishing books, but it wasn't that simple. As I entered middle school and high school, I thought less about writing and more about things like clothes, friends, cheerleading, and boys. I decided that writing took too long and I quit (the first of many times that I have quit!)

When I was in high school, one of my teachers, Father Jerome, gave my English class an assignment that did not interest me. Our county college published a book with work from residents and students each year. Our assignment was to write a poem by the end of the week. Determined not to participate, I spent each day doodling in my notebook. At the end of each class, Father Jerome would come up and remind me that time was running out. I would then tell him that I couldn't think of anything and therefore, would not be able to turn in a poem. By the time Thursday rolled around, I thought I was in the clear. Then, Father Jerome quietly walked up to my desk and whispered these words:

"If you don't turn in a poem, you will no longer be a cheerleader. Have a nice day."

Annoyed that I was forced to write a poem, I wrote one about how hard it was to write poetry. It started like this:

It seems impossible to me, to write a piece of poetry.
The word itself must be a curse, 'cause I can't even
write a verse!

My poem went on to complain, in detail, about how horrible writing a poem can be and I assured myself that he would hate it. I can't begin to explain my anger, when I received a certified letter telling me my poem was selected and would be published. Later, that year, Father Jerome told me that I had a wonderful gift and I should not waste it. When I look back now, I wish I had listened.

You see, it took me years to start writing again, and when I did, I was rusty. Right before I graduated from college, I bought a word processor (half typewriter and half computer). For the first time in my life, even though I really wanted to write, I couldn't think of anything to write about. So, for a year, the dust on the word processor grew thicker and thicker.

When I graduated from college, I was hired in my hometown of Trenton, New Jersey as a second grade teacher. Being a new teacher took up so much time, that I never even thought about writing. At the end of my first year, I was assigned a fourth grade class for the following school year. It took two months with my fourth graders to realize that, not only did I want to write, but that I wanted to write for children.

So eight picture books and two chapter books later, I am now writing a book about writing because I know what it is like to be stuck for an idea and I know that you aren't always in the mood to write. This book is dedicated to all of the kids who love to write and those who would rather wash windows than write a story. Hopefully, you will all be motivated to pick up a pen or sit at a computer and write, whether its for yourself or to share with the world.

Answers to Your Questions

Before we get started, I'm sure you have plenty of questions and I always like to get the questions out of the way first! So borrowing some of the many questions kids ask me when I speak at their schools, we'll begin.

Why don't people like to write anymore?

I don't think people dislike writing so much as I think people do not feel that they have the time. Think about it, three hundred years ago, early Americans had so many chores to complete, just to survive, that writing was their recreation. They didn't have television, movies, video games, malls, and all of the other modern luxuries and time-saving products we have today. Three hundred years later, thanks to technology, life has become much easier and compared to television, movies, and video games, writing has become the chore.

Why should I write?

Maybe the question should be, *why not?* Writing is just putting your thoughts on paper, just as speaking is saying your thoughts out loud. When you write, however, you have a chance to fix your thoughts before sharing them. You can organize what you want to say and listen to it before anyone else does. Writing gives you what speaking can't, a *Do-Over*. If you don't like the way it sounds, you can always erase it and start over again.

Why write if I don't want to be an Author?

That's like saying why play baseball if I'm not going to play in the major leagues? Sure, some people go on to become professional writers, but it doesn't mean everyone can't enjoy writing. Whether it becomes your career or just something you enjoy doing, one thing is true; the more you write, the better your writing and speaking become. (That's right, your speaking will also improve!)

Why is writing boring?

Writing never has to be boring. If your writing seems like it is, take a look at what you're writing about. If you are writing a fiction story, you can make it as exciting as you like. Be creative, be fun, and always leave the reader (even if its you) wanting more. If you are writing about a real topic, make sure that the topic is interesting. The best writing always starts with a strong topic.

What should I write about?

Whether you write for fun or for a living, you should always write about topics that you find interesting. Since I am a horrible cook, I would never write a cookbook. However, since I love to travel, I enjoy writing about different places. In order for your writing to be exciting, you need to be excited. You can write short stories, poems, songs, plays, recipes, articles, biographies, or a journal. The list is endless!

Why don't publishers publish kids' work?

Ah, that's a question that I asked myself over and over again when I was a kid, and back then there were virtually no opportunities for kids. Nowadays, things are much different. There are dozens and dozens of magazines that not only publish kids' work, they look for it. Because I felt so strongly about giving children the opportunity to experience becoming published authors, I reserved two pages in all of my children's picture books so that kids could send in their stories or artwork. The first, second, and third place winners even have their work published. So far, 27 children have become published authors and illustrators. The opportunities are out there and I've included a chapter to help you find them and to help you prepare to submit your work.

Is it fun to be an author?

I guess that depends upon your definition of fun. For me, being an author is amazing, especially since I dreamed about it when I was eight years old. In my life, I have had hard jobs, from waitressing to selling bridal gowns to being a nanny and teaching. Of all of my jobs, I enjoy writing the most, with teaching being a close second. One of the reasons I love it so much is because a part of my job involves School Author Visits and Writing Workshops. I travel to 60-70 schools, each year, all over the country, speaking to kids just like yourselves. In a way, I am still teaching, but as an author,

I teach thousands of kids each year. I also enjoy watching a story grow from a small kernel of an idea into a book and seeing my name on the cover (it still gives me chills!). As a mother of two young children, I write when its convenient and spend much more time with my family. So, yes, it is fun, and amazing, and always interesting.

Is being an author hard?

I'll tell you what my mom always told me and that is anything worthwhile is hard at times. This, of course is true in writing. There are times when I am so frustrated or stuck for an idea or an ending, that I'm ready to throw my computer out of the window (luckily my office is on the first floor). Those are times, however, when you need to walk away and stop forcing ideas to develop. When I'm really stuck, I put my kids in the car and take them to the park. It's amazing what a little time away will do.

Are editors mean?

Poor editors, they have such a reputation! Actually, editors have a very important job and the success of a book is resting upon their shoulders. They not only look for mistakes, they also tell the author what parts are strong and what parts are not so strong. Of course, as an author, we'd like to think that our stories are perfect, but even the best authors know that you can't be your own editor and we appreciate their work. As students, you work with your own editors everyday...your teachers. Editors do the same things your teachers do, checking your work and making it better; they just don't give out stickers!

What's the hardest part of being an author?

Coming up with fresh, new ideas is always a challenge. Sometimes they just pop into your head, but other times, it's a struggle. Another issue is time. Since authors do not report to work, it is very easy to become distracted and other people seem to forget that even though you are working at home, you are still working. Of course, working from a home office with a three year old son is the biggest challenge. This is especially true when you find out that the First Lady has selected one of your books (*Chumpkin*) as a favorite and you are on the phone with the White House and your darling son is yelling that he has to go potty!

What were your favorite books?

When I was a little kid, I loved rhyming books, which is why my picture books rhyme. I always enjoyed the clever way an author could tell a story, using rhyming words and listening to the rhythm as they were read to me. My favorite picture book author was Dr. Suess. As I got older and started reading chapter books, my favorite series was the Trixie Belden Mysteries. I also loved the Little House on The Prairie books.

What advice would you give a young author?

I've always believed that the best way to become a great writer is to read as much as you can and write frequently. Like most things in life, the more you practice, the better you will become. Having said that, I also encourage writers to write about what they know and what interests them, to start off slow, and to go back and read things they have written. I definitely recommend keeping a journal, whether it's about things you do with your friends or family, or just about your feelings. One day, when you are older, you will be so happy that you have a record of your younger days and if you have children, they will cherish it.

Great Writers Are Everywhere

Ask any kid to name a great writer and more than half will say J.K. Rowling. While they are correct, writers are everywhere. Some are very famous, most are not, but they all have one thing in common. When you think of writing as an occupation, don't limit yourself to only those who write books. Here is a list of just some of the occupations that require writing.

❏ Reporter/Columnist
Many writers write for newspapers and magazines.
Their writing is usually related to the things they enjoy, including sports, cooking, business, and humor.

❏ Copywriter
When you watch the news, someone has written down what the anchor person is saying and that person is the copywriter.

❏ Advertising
For every advertisement from radio and television to magazines and newspapers to billboards, someone had to think of and write the words you are reading.
Writing is a key part of advertising.

❏ Songwriters
Music is everywhere in our lives and behind the words to every song you hear is a songwriter.

❑ Screenwriters

For every television show or movie, there will be a team of writers who use their words to make us laugh or cry or think about something new.

❑ Lawyers

Even though we don't always understand what they are writing, lawyers spend a great deal of time writing.

❑ Chefs

For a chef, writing a recipe is the same as when a song writer writes a song.

❑ Educator

Whether you are a preschool teacher or a college professor, writing will be become a large part of your job.

❑ Doctor

Doctors write more than prescriptions. They spend a great deal of time writing notes and charts about their patients.

❑ Managers

Whether someone manages a clothing store, an auto parts store, or a bank, there will always be plenty of reports and letters to write.

As you can see by this small sampling of people who write everyday, writing plays an important part in the world. You don't need to write the Great American Novel to enjoy writing. If you start young, you'll be prepared for the writing you will surely do in whatever field you choose.

In The Beginning
Pre-writing

As I mentioned, one of the most important things you can do, as a writer, is choose your topic carefully. You want a topic that you are interested in, that others would be interested in, and you want to make sure you have enough to write about.

If you are stuck, make a list of things you enjoy, places you have gone, or places you would like to go. Go over the list and see what excites you the most. Think about special occasions, holidays, traditions, or things that have gone wrong. Nothing seems to make people laugh more than a story of mishaps, including flat tires, alarm clocks that never went off, and unexpected guests. People enjoy stories about mishaps and misunderstandings because they are things they can relate to and understand.

Here's an example of a list of general topics:

1. Summer reunion
2. Baseball games
3. Amusement parks
4. Trip to Florida
5. When dad locked the keys in the car

Once you make your list, a topic may jump right off the page. If it doesn't, don't worry. Next to each topic, write a few notes about it. It doesn't have to be much and it doesn't have to be neat (as long as you can understand it). Try to think of the funny, sad, or exciting moments.

For example, we'll write about amusement parks.

Topic: Amusement Park

Most people have either been to an actual amusement park, a carnival, or a fair (or have at least seen the commercials). They are all very similar and people can relate to them. They are exciting and filled with many things to write about.

Now, like many topics, there are many, many things you could discuss in a story about amusement parks and you do not want to write about every single one. When people do this, their stories tend to be scattered all over the place. The following is an example of the kind of scattered story my fourth grade students would turn in:

Last Saturday, my family was supposed to go to the mall, but we didn't. My dad got a flat tire on the way home from the bank and he didn't have a spare. My mom was really mad because she always tells him he should have one. Last year my grandmom had a flat tire. I love going over my grandmom's house because she cooks better than my mom. Last time we ate over she had fried chicken and macaroni and cheese. I love macaroni and cheese, but I really love chocolate cake. Mike's mom makes the best chocolate cake in the world. I told her she should enter it in a contest. I once won a math contest, but they gave us a ribbon instead of a trophy. One day I want to have a big trophy. If I had a big trophy I would bring it to school and show my teacher. My teacher is nice and has straight hair.

Now, as you can see, that story goes from topic to topic, and include's anything that popped into the writer's head. **That is not the type of story you want to write.** You want your story to be what editors call *tight*. See below.

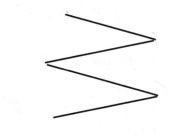

Tight Story   **Zig Zag Story**

You don't want your topic to be all over the place, you want it follow a straight line. Whatever topic you begin writing about should be the topic you are writing about at the end of your story.

Once you have a topic that you are happy with, you want to make a list of ideas that stick to your topic.

Topic: Amusement Parks
Ideas:
> **1. rides**
> **2. games**
> **3. food**
> **4. shows**
> **5. characters**
> **6. stores**

Your list doesn't have to be huge, just enough to get the juices flowing in your brain!

After you've finished making a list of ideas, you will want to study those ideas carefully. If you write about all of them in one story, your story won't be tight. Decide, from your list of ideas, what you would really like to write about and that will become part of your topic.

Now if you are like me, you love rides, so for this story, we'll pick rides.

Topic: Amusement Parks
Ideas:
> 1. rides ☒
> 2. games
> 3. food
> 4. shows
> 5. characters
> 6. stores

New Topic: Amusement Park Rides

So far, you are doing great. You have narrowed down a huge topic into a more manageable one. Of course, you now want to take a good look at the topic of amusement park rides. If you have ever been to an amusement park, you know that they have tons of rides. This could get tricky if you don't decide what type of rides you are going to discuss.

This time, instead of making a list, use a word web to help you decide what kind of rides you would like to write about. The following word web helps you put all of those rides into categories.

Word Web

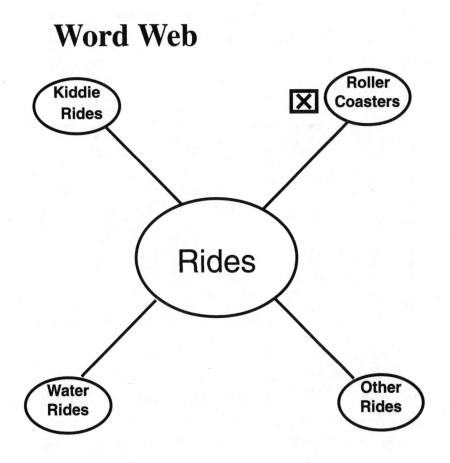

Once you can take a good at your word web, think about each idea and how much you would have to write about it. Since I love roller coasters, I would pick roller coasters as my next topic and I would write about:

Topic: Amusement Parks/Rides/Roller Coasters

Congratulations! You have selected your topic and that should be a load off of your mind. It's time to start pre-writing. Before you begin, however, make sure you are still interested in your topic.

What if I change my mind?

A very good question. That's one of the best parts of being the author...you're the boss. You can always change your mind and start again!

Once you are sure about your topic, you may want to get right to the writing. **STOP!** If you are not working on a deadline or sitting in a classroom, put down your papers and go outside and play. That's right, with permission, go out and run around and get some fresh air. Clear your mind and stop thinking so hard and you will be surprised at how many ideas pop into your head! You may want to continue when you are finished playing or you may want to wait a day or two. Either way, you never want to force creativity!

When you do get back to work, you'll want to think of some details that go with your topic. Since our topic is roller coaster rides at amusement parks, we should think of some simple, little descriptions. A fun way to do this is a mimi word web.

Mini Word Web

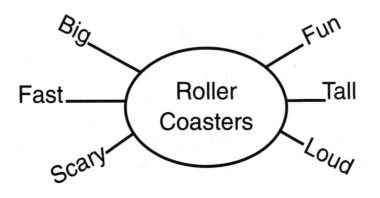

Now, you may have noticed that these words are kind of simple. There is a very good reason to list these little words. Once they are on your list...you are not allowed to use them in your story! That's right, these words are overused, boring, and will not interest your reader. Avoid them!

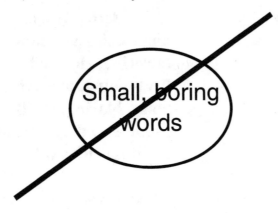

Now, I probably know your next question. I bet you were going to ask where you could find bigger, more exciting words, weren't you? Okay, turn the page and I'll tell you.

The Better Word Book

or as smart types refer to it, the Thesaurus!

If you have ever used a thesaurus, you know just how important this book is to a writer. As an author, it is probably my most worn out book and the one I use most often. It's also one of my favorites.

A thesaurus works like a dictionary, but rather than giving you a definition, it provides you with words that mean the same or the opposite of a particular word. You remember synonyms and antonyms from second grade, right?

Make a list using the small, boring words from your mini word web. Then, look up synonyms for each word. It may take you fifteen minutes, but it's easy to do and trust me, it will make your writing much more interesting.

Boring Words	Better Words
big	huge, colossal, immense
tall	towering, elevated
scary	frightening, terrifying
loud	noisy, blaring, shrill
fast	rapid, speedy, swift, quick
fun	exciting, enjoyable

As you can see, the better words really are better and using them in your writing would make your writing infinitely more interesting (if you're not sure what infinitely means, go ahead and grab a thesaurus). When you are armed with a list of better words, you are ready to map out your story.

Think Twist

The Straight Arrow Map With A Twist

Each year, I travel all over the country, visiting schools and meeting children. It is one of the perks of being an author and gives me a chance to visit places many people never even knew existed. Traveling is exciting but there is always a possibility of getting lost. Even though I know where I'm starting and I know where I'd like to end up, things don't always go according to plan. The best way to travel from one point to another is to use a map. Whether you're traveling across Italy or trying to find the arcade at the mall, you've got a better chance of reaching your destination if you use a map.

Surprisingly, it's the same thing when I write a story. I usually know where it will begin and how I would like it to end, but getting from point A (the beginning) to point B (the end) is a bit tricky. To keep my story on track, I always use a straight arrow map. It helps me connect all of the events that move the story forward. It also keeps me focused. Without a map, it is very, very easy to veer off-track and end up with a scattered, zig-zag story.

The only difference between a road map and a straight arrow map is the Twist. The twist is that little something that the reader doesn't see coming and makes them want to keep turning the pages. I'll show you first and then I'll explain.

Straight Arrow Map   **Straight Arrow Map**
                                  with a Twist

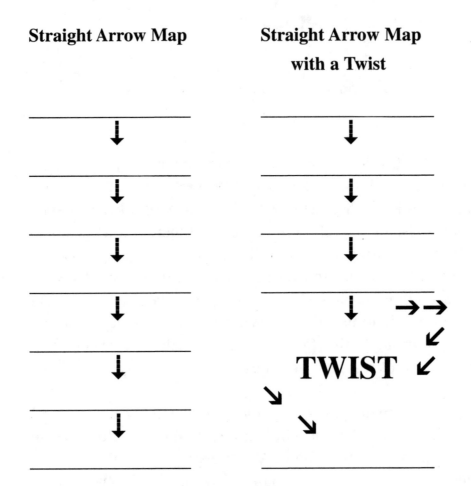

Now, you may be wondering why, after telling you to keep your story tight and following a straight line, I would then tell you to add a TWIST! The answer is simple. If your story follows a completely straight line it will, no doubt, be boring and very predictable. The reader will know the ending before he or she even gets close to it. A twist is different than the scattered story a few pages back. A twist is something you plan. It is like a strategy. You think about your story and add something that is somewhat realistic to surprise the reader and add excitement. A scattered story, on the other hand, is when you start to ramble and your story goes wildly off-course.

The trick to creating a great twist is to create something believable. Your twist should be something that:

- ◆ sticks to your topic
- ◆ is something unexpected
- ◆ could possibly happen

If your story is about a race car driver, a funny twist could be that he thinks he won the race, but doesn't realize that he still has one lap to go as the others race past him. A touching twist could be that as he is about to complete the last lap and win, he sees his little daughter has fallen and is crying in the stands so he pulls over to comfort his daughter. A Martian landing on the track wouldn't be the best twist!

Twists come in all shapes and sizes and the only limit is your imagination. They can be happy, sad, funny, or touching. The only rule is that they are unexpected.

When it's time to start mapping your story, think about the characters and the setting. Decide if the characters have any traits that would lend themselves to a great twist. Perhaps the main character is forgetful or shy. If that is the case, the twist may involve this person doing something that is considered to be *out of character*, or something he or she wouldn't usually do. In your twist, this person may remember something very important that everyone else forgot or may become the most outgoing character in the story.

Another thing you should keep in mind is that creating a map is still a part of pre-writing and does not require full sentences or even full words. Feel free to abbreviate.

Let's map our amusement park topic:

<u>Without a Twist</u>

Boy wants to visit <u>A</u>musement <u>P</u>ark

↓

Boy is excited about 1st time riding <u>R</u>oller <u>C</u>oasters

↓

In car, boy goes on and on about R.C.

↓

Family pulls into A.P. parking lot

↓

First, he hears the R.C.

↓

Next, he sees the R.C.

↓

He decides which R.C. to ride first.

↓

He rides the R.C.

↓

The End

If this story followed a straight arrow map, it would be the dullest, most boring story ever. The reader would say one of the three things you never want a reader to say when finished with your story:

Big Deal!   So What?   Who Cares?

Now, let's spice it up, a bit!

<u>With a Twist</u>

Boy wants to visit Amusement Park

↓

Excited about 1st time riding Roller Coasters

↓

In car, boy goes on and on about R.C.

↓

Little old <u>G</u>rand<u>M</u>om says R.C. is too fast/dangerous

↓

Boy ignores GM and says all of his friends ride R.C.

↓

Family pulls into A.P. parking lot

↓

Boy hears R.C.

↓

Boy sees R.C

↓

Decides which R.C. to ride first

↓

GM goes w/ him to make sure he's buckled in   ↩

Now, here comes the first TWIST...

RC pulls in, boy doesn't move, R.C. leaves

↓

Next R.C. pulls in, boy doesn't move, R.C. leaves

↓

↳ Boy chickens out, so GM pushes him to the exit

And, here comes the second TWIST...

Boy, disappointed, turns around and hears "Look at Me!"

GM is riding the RD!

Now, let's take a look at the two very different stories. In the first one, the boy is excited about riding a roller coaster for the first time. As his family pulls into the parking lot, before he can even see the roller coasters, he hears them. This is a great place to describe how roller coasters sound. You can write about the screeching wheels along the metal tracks, the slow, clicking sounds as the roller coaster climbs the first hill, the thunderous sounds as the cars rise and fall, or the people screaming with fear and excitement.

Notice how good descriptions can make the reader feel like he or she is also at the amusement park.

As he gets closer, the boy can describe all of the roller coasters he sees. He can tell the reader how colossal they are, how they tower over all of the other rides, how each one is a different color, etc.

Once he decides which roller coaster he will ride, if we stick to the straight arrow map, he will logically ride the roller coaster and the story will end. There's only one problem. This would be one of the most boring stories in the world, maybe in the galaxy. The reader would be thinking, big deal, so a kid wanted to ride a roller coaster and he did. So what? Who cares?

With the second story, a few adjustments make a world of difference. The first thing we did was to add a *foil*. Since the boy is so excited about riding the roller coasters, we added a very old, very worried grandmother. She does not think the roller coaster is safe and this makes the boy even more determined to prove her wrong. That one adjustment sets the stage for the twist.

The story is the same as the first one until we reach the part where he is next in line. In the first story he simply rides the roller coaster, ending the story. In the second story, he is standing there as the roller coaster pulls into the station. The people on board get off, everyone else gets on, the roller coaster leaves, but our hero is still standing there. Another roller coaster pulls in, people get off, people get on, and he is still standing there. The **First Twist** is that the boy has chickened out, he is too afraid to even move. So the grandmother starts to push him toward the exit. Disappointed with himself, he turns around and hears (the **Second Twist**) his grandmother holler, "Look at me!" as *she* rides the roller coaster!

Tahdah! Our main character, the boy who went on and on about how he was going to ride the roller coasters, chickened out and his grandmother who was deathly afraid of them, hopped on at the last moment. This is a twist and it is something that your readers will not expect. It will also make them want to read more. Good job.

Now, the next step would be to write your first draft, but I think you've done enough for today. Go get some fresh air and play, with your parents' permission, of course!

First Draft of Many

Repeat after me, "I am never finished writing a story after the first draft!" "I am never finished writing a story after the first draft!" "I am never finished writing a story after the first draft!" "I am never finished writing a story after the first draft!"

Great! Once you understand that it takes more than one draft to write a great story, you are on your way. Sometimes kids think that writing a rough draft is just something their teachers or parents make them do to torture them. The truth of the matter is that every writer, from new writers to very, very famous writers use several drafts to create a good story.

The trick to writing a good first draft is to stick to your map and use your better words. You want to write your ideas down, as you would in your final draft, in sentences, with capital letters and punctuation. The only difference between the two is that you will go back and make changes and fix things.

Here are some tips for getting started:
1. Find a quiet place to work.
2. Keep all of your prewriting material close to you.
3. As you write, keep checking your map.
4. Don't worry about spelling (right now)!

··

The First Draft

Tuesday was the day I have been waiting for all summer long. My parents were finaly taking us to Ride World and I was ready to ride the roller coasters. As usual, my grandmom was coming to hold our stuff and watch my little sister.

I was really, really, really excited about riding the roller coasters and I talked about it the whole way there. My grandmom told me that she thout roller coasters were too high and too fast and too dangerous. I told her they weren't and I told her that all of my friends ride roller coasters. She asked me if I would jump off of a brige because my friends were jumping. I decided to listen to my CD player.

When we pulled into the lot at ride world, I couldn't even see the roller coasters, but I could hear the screeching of the wheels on the metal tracks and the people screaming. It sounded great.

As we got closer, I could see the biggest roller coaster in the park, The Tonsil Tamer. It was enormous and towered over the other rides. I also saw the Spider Legs roller coaster. Tommy always goes on the Tonsil Tamer, so I headed that way.

Just before I got in line, my grandmom said that she wanted to walk up with me to make sure I was buckled into the car. I was humilated and asked my mom to tell her no. My mom ignoed me and I walked up the stairs with my grandmom and we waited in line.

It took twenty minutes to get tot he front of the line and stood in the spot for the first car. In a few seconds, the roller coaster came howling into the station and the riders got off. Everyone in line got on and the roller coaster pulled out off the station, clicking its way up the first big hill.

I was still standing in line. I don't know why, but my feet seemed to be glued to the koncrete floor. When the next one pulled in, everyone got off, new people got on, and it left the station. Sadly, I was still standing there and the people behind me in the line started to yell.

As the next train pulled in, my grandmother waited for the people to get off and pushed me through to the other side, toward the exit. I was mad and sad that after all the talk, I was too afraid to get on.

Just as I reached the exit, I heard a familiar voice yell, "Hey, look at me!" I turned around to find my grandmother, buckled into the roller coaster, waveing with both hands! The roller coast took off, with my grandmom in the front seat.

●●●●●●●●●●●●●●●●●●●●●●●●●●●●●

Now, our first draft looks like a final draft, but there are always ways to make a story better. Before you start to make changes, however, I have some advice. Once you have completed your first draft, take it, put it in a drawer, and go outside and get some fresh air (with your parents permission, of course)!

Kids always look at me funny and some ask the obvious questions, what if I'm not allowed to go outside or what if it's raining? Well, of course, I would never want anyone to disobey their parents and I know you would never do that anyway. I would also never advise you to go outside in bad weather, so if going outside isn't possible, do something inside as long as you are NOT WORKING ON YOUR STORY!

The idea is to give your brain a break and stop thinking about your story. When you go back to revise it (by the way, that means fix your story), you want it to sound fresh. You want to be able to hear the things that need to be changed and actually see the mistakes. So whether you ride your bike, jump rope, or eat an apple, do something to take your mind off of your story.

> When I was writing **Where Do Snowmen Go**, I put it away after the first draft and went outside to play in the snow with my little kids. While we were playing, I got some great new ideas and I wasn't even trying to think of any!

Beating The Red Pen

Beating Your Teacher To The Mistakes

So many of my own students thought of editing as boring and they hated to revise and edit their work. I knew I had to think of a way to get them interested and I also knew how they loved to win anything. I decided to challenge them to find the mistakes before my red pen did!

My students loved the idea of beating me at something and by the end of each year, they could have been hired as New York Times editors. Of course, they didn't start off beating me, it takes time to learn how to find mistakes and make stories better. To make it easier, I taught them some editor tricks and some writer tricks.

Before I tell you the tricks, let's make sure you know what editing is all about. There are really two parts to editing your work. I'm guessing that the first part is probably not what you think, since most kids want to dive right in for the mistakes.

The truth is, editing is two parts:

1. Listening to a story to decide if it is interesting, uses better words, and is well written.
2. Finding and cleaning up the mistakes.

So many kids forget all about Number 1 and it is very, very, very, very, very, very, very important! Get the picture? The key to good editing is making sure you check the content of the story (what it says) *and clean up the mistakes.*

Remember, someone can write a story that has no mistakes and it can be the most painfully boring story you have ever read. At the same time, someone can write a beautiful story that is filled with mistakes, making it difficult to enjoy.

When you have given your brain a break from your story, you may begin editing. Here are the steps I use when revising my stories:

Step 1 - Read your story out loud.

When you read your story silently, it is very hard to hear how it will sound to someone else. If you read it out loud, you will hear things like using the same word too many times or forgetting words. You'll also pick up on sentences that are too, too, too, too, too long!

Read your story out loud, one time, without stopping to change anything.

Step 2 - Ask yourself the hard questions?

Is it interesting?
Does it make sense?
Did I stick to my plan?
Did I use a good twist?
Did I use some words too many times?

After you think about those questions, read it out loud, once more. This time, I want you to stop after each paragraph. When you reach the end of a paragraph, make your changes that you need to make. You may want to change a simple word to a better word. You may want to change a word you have said over and over and over! This is usually the time when I remember something I forgot to add.

When you have listened to each paragraph, make your changes then write a second draft with the changes. If you are writing on paper, this means re-writing the story. If you are writing on a computer, it means adding or deleting items.

••••••••••••••••••••••••••••••••••••

Revising the First Draft

Tuesday was the day I have been waiting for all summer ~~long~~. My parents were finaly taking us to ride world and I was ready to ride the roller coasters. As usual, my grandmom was coming to hold our things and watch my little sister.

I was ~~really~~, ~~really~~, really excited about riding the roller coasters and I talked about it the whole way there. My grandmom told me that she thout roller coasters were too high, ~~and~~ too fast, and too dangerous. I told her they weren't and ~~I told her~~ that all of my friends ride roller coasters. She asked me if I would jump off of a brige because my friends were jumping. I decided to listen to my CD player.

When we pulled into the lot at ride world, I couldn't ~~even~~ see the roller coasters, but I could hear the screeching of the wheels on the metal tracks and the people screaming. It sounded great.

As we got closer, I could see the biggest roller coaster in the park, The Tonsil Tamer. It was enormous and towered over the other rides. I also saw the Spider Legs roller ~~coaster. Tommy always goes on the Tonsil Tamer, so I hea~~ded that way.

Just before I got in line, my grandmom said that she wanted to walk up with me to make sure I was buckled into the car. I was humilated and **begged** my mom to tell her no. My mom ignoed me and I walked up the **steep** stairs with my grandmom and we waited in line.

It took twenty minutes to get tot he front of the line and **I** stood in the spot for the first car. In a few seconds, the roller coaster came howling into the station and the riders got off. Everyone in line got on and the roller coaster pulled out off the station, clicking its way up the first big hill.

Unfortunately, I was still standing in line. I don't know why, but my feet seemed to be glued to the koncrete floor. When the next one pulled in, everyone got off, new people got on, and it left the station. Sadly, I was still standing there and the people behind me ~~in the line~~ started to yell.

As the next train pulled in, my grandmother waited for the people to get off and pushed me through to the other side, toward the exit. I was **furious with myself** and **disappointed** that after all the talk, I was too **terrified** to get on.

Just as I reached the exit, I heard a familiar voice yell, "Hey, look at me!" I turned around to find my **little, old** grandmother, buckled into the roller coaster, waveing with both hands! The roller coast took off, with my grandmom in the front seat.

● ●

Now, you can see that some things have been changed, some words deleted, and some words added. Hopefully, you have also noticed that we didn't correct grammar mistakes, like spelling, capital letters, and punctuation. Don't worry, we'll get to it later. Right now, we are making the story sound better by taking out things that don't belong, like a sentence about Tommy, who is never even mentioned. We're also adding some forgotten and better words (the words in bold type).

You are well on your way to Beating The Red Pen! Now, you can rewrite your story so you will have your second draft. Here is your second draft with the changes you have made so far:

● ●

Second Draft

Tuesday was the day I have been waiting for all summer. My parents were finaly taking us to ride world and I was ready to ride the roller coasters. As usual, my grandmom was coming to hold our things and watch my little sister.

I was really excited about riding the roller coasters and I talked about it the whole way there. My grandmom told me that she thout roller coasters were too high, too fast, and too dangerous. I told her they weren't and that all of my friends ride roller coasters. She asked me if I would jump off of a brige because my friends were jumping. I decided to listen to my CD player.

When we pulled into the lot at ride world, I couldn't see the roller coasters, but I could hear the screeching of the wheels on the metal tracks and the people screaming. It sounded great.

As we got closer, I could see the biggest roller coaster in the park, The Tonsil Tamer. It was enormous and towered over the other rides. I also saw the Spider Legs roller coaster.

Just before I got in line, my grandmom said that she wanted to walk up with me to make sure I was buckled into the car. I was humilated and begged my mom to tell her no. My mom ignoed me and I walked up the steep stairs with my grandmom and we waited in line.

It took twenty minutes to get tot he front of the line and I stood in the spot for the first car. In a few seconds, the roller coaster came howling into the station and the riders got off. Everyone in line got on and the roller coaster pulled out off the station, clicking its way up the first big hill.

Unfortunately, I was still standing in line. I don't know why, but my feet seemed to be glued to the koncrete floor. When the next one pulled in, everyone got off, new people got on, and it left the station. Sadly, I was still standing there and the people behind me started to yell.

As the next train pulled in, my grandmother waited for the people to get off and pushed me through to the other side, toward the exit. I was furious with myself and disappointed that after all the talk, I was too terrified to get on.

Just as I reached the exit, I heard a familiar voice yell, "Hey, look at me!" I turned around to find my little, old grandmother, buckled into the roller coaster, waveing with both hands! The roller coast took off, with my grandmom in the front seat.

● ●

Now, I'm sure you know the drill. When you are finished revising your first draft and creating your second draft, put it away and do something else!

> Next time you begin to complain about writing, remember, math teachers don't have you stop and play in the middle of a word problem, do they?

After you feel like you've taken enough time, you can start to find the mistakes in your second draft. It sounds easy, but sometimes it can get really tricky!

The first thing I look for is the misspelled words. Unfortunately, they are the hardest mistakes to find and you may think that it would be easier finding green jelly beans in Ireland! Spelling mistakes are the sneakiest of all mistakes.

Eyes Playing Tricks On You?

Actually, they are! Once your mind knows a story, your eyes cannot keep up when you are looking for misspelled words. Instead of checking each word, your eyes skim across the page and see how the word should be spelled, not how you spelled it!
I can't tell you how often I have checked a story 12 times and an editor still finds some misspelled words.

Now, you may be wondering how anyone finds spelling mistakes. When I visit schools to teach writing workshops, many students think they know the answer:

SPELL CHECK

Unfortunately, the answer is not spell check. In fact, I would like to repeat after me:

SPELL CHECK IS NOT MY FRIEND!
SPELL CHECK IS NOT MY FRIEND!
SPELL CHECK IS NOT MY FRIEND!
SPELL CHECK IS NOT MY FRIEND!
SPELL CHECK IS NOT MY FRIEND!

In case you're not familiar with SPELL CHECK, I will explain it to you. SPELL CHECK is part of a computer program. While computers are wonderful, they cannot think and do not have brains. Sure, they're fast, but they only do what people tell them to do.

A long, long time ago, when I was your age, we dreamed a machine would be invented that could magically find and fix misspelled words. We imagined how much easier life would be without those nagging spelling errors. Then people started using computers at home and we were introduced to the wonderful world of SPELL CHECK. It would be easy, just type your story, press a button, and presto...all of your words are spelled perfectly.

Unfortunately, that isn't exactly how it worked out. Now, don't get me wrong, I love SPELL CHECK, but I don't rely on it and I know that it is not my friend. A good friend will never let you down and SPELL CHECK will. Here's what happens.

You're busy writing a wonderful story and you're ready to check your second draft. You smile as you hit the button for SPELL CHECK, which is now busy reading each word to see if it is spelled correctly. But, alas, there is a problem. Look at the sentence below and see what you think.

I went tot he store.

It seems easy enough to figure out that you typed a space in the wrong place and that your sentence makes no sense. But guess what, SPELL CHECK is clapping for you right now because you have no spelling mistakes.

That's right, SPELL CHECK is ready to congratulate you on your fine spelling. Why, you ask? It's simple. The program is designed to check for one thing, misspelled words. Check out that sentence and you will see that every word is spelled correctly. **I** is spelled correctly, **went** is spelled correctly, **tot** (a small child) is spelled correctly, **he** is spelled correctly, and **store** is spelled correctly. Good job!

Wait a minute, it doesn't make sense! It should be:

I went to the store.

But remember, it isn't SPELL CHECK'S job to make sure your work makes sense. Its only job is to check each word, one at a time. It has no idea what you are trying to say and may even tell you that your name is spelled wrong! Unfortunately, it's very easy to type fast and misspell a word that turns out to be another word. That is why you can use SPELL CHECK, you just can't rely on it!

Let me guess what your next questions is, if my eyes play tricks on my mind and SPELL CHECK is a fair weather friend, how am I supposed to find the spelling mistakes? Well, you could do what the editors do...

Read each line backwards!

Don't forget that the reason your eyes can play tricks on your mind is because you know the story and the rhythm. If you read each line backwards, even as the author, you won't know which words come next. There will be no rhythm and you will force your eyes to check out each and every word.

For instance, here is a line from my picture book called **<u>Chumpkin</u>**:

←←←←←←←←←←←←←←←←←←←←←←←←←←←

If only they would put me on a fat-free pumpkin diet, I'd
←←←←←←←←←←←←←←←←←←←←←←←←←←←

finally hear those magic words, "Hey, Mister can I buy it?"
←←←←←←←←←←←←←←←←←←←←←←←←←←←

I'm the author of that book and I can say that story in my sleep. If you placed a misspelled word in that book, I would probably never find it. So I would read it moving from the right to the left and it would sound like this:

I'd diet pumpkin fat-free a on me put would they only If it buy can Mister Hey words magic those hear finally

This is how editors look for and, more importantly, find, misspelled words. Now that you know how it's done, go to the second draft on page 44 and check for spelling, capital letter, and punctuation mistakes. I'll underline all of these mistakes from the second draft.

● ●

Second Draft corrections

Tuesday was the day I have been waiting for all summer. My parents were **<u>finaly</u>** taking us to <u>r</u>ide <u>w</u>orld and I was ready to ride the roller coasters. As usual, my grandmom was coming to hold our things and watch my little sister.

I was really excited about riding the roller coasters and I talked about it the whole way there. My grandmom told me that she **thout** roller coasters were too high, too fast, and too dangerous. I told her they weren't and that all of my friends ride roller coasters. She asked me if I would jump off of a **brige** because my friends were jumping. I decided to listen to my CD player.

When we pulled into the lot at **r**ide **w**orld, I couldn't see the roller coasters, but I could hear the screeching of the wheels on the metal tracks and the people screaming. It sounded great.

As we got closer, I could see the biggest roller coaster in the park, The Tonsil Tamer. It was enormous and towered over the other rides. I also saw the Spider Legs roller coaster.

Just before I got in line, my grandmom said that she wanted to walk up with me to make sure I was buckled into the car. I was **humilated** and begged my mom to tell her no. My mom **ignoed** me and I walked up the steep stairs with my grandmom and we waited in line.

It took twenty minutes to get **tot he** front of the line and I stood in the spot for the first car. In a few seconds, the roller coaster came howling into the station and the riders got off. Everyone in line got on and the roller coaster pulled out **off** the station, clicking its way up the first big hill.

Unfortunately, I was still standing in line. I don't know why, but my feet seemed to be glued to the **koncrete** floor. When the next one pulled in, everyone got off, new people got on, and it left the station. Sadly, I was still standing there and the people behind me started to yell.

As the next train pulled in, my grandmother waited for the people to get off and pushed me through to the other side, toward the exit. I was furious with myself and disappointed that after all the talk, I was too terrified to get on.

Just as I reached the exit, I heard a familiar voice yell, "Hey, look at me!" I turned around to find my little, old grandmother, buckled into the roller coaster, **waveing** with both hands! The roller **coast** took off, with my grandmom in the front seat.

● ●

Now, I'm sure you already guessed what I'm going to say next. You probably think I am going to tell you to go out and play. SURPRISE, not this time! Instead of playing, find a parent, teacher, brother, sister, aunt, uncle, or friend to read your story.

Every good writer needs at least 6 eyes!

Before you go to the trouble of writing your final (last) draft, have two other people read your story. Insist that they be completely honest with you. Ask them to check for mistakes and to also give you their feedback on the story. Do they like it? Was it interesting? How was the beginning? How was the middle? How was the end? Did they want to know more when they finished reading it?

Now you are ready to give your story a catchy title and prepare your final draft.

Roller Coaster Blues

by X. Cellent Writer

Tuesday was the day I have been waiting for all summer. My parents were finally taking us to Ride World and I was ready to ride the roller coasters. As usual, my grandmom was coming to hold our things and watch my little sister.

I was really excited about riding the roller coasters and I talked about it the whole way there. My grandmom told me that she thought roller coasters were too high, too fast, and too dangerous. I told her they weren't and that all of my friends ride roller coasters. She asked me if I would jump off of a bridge because my friends were jumping. I decided to listen to my CD player.

When we pulled into the lot at Ride World, I couldn't see the roller coasters, but I could hear the screeching of the wheels on the metal tracks and the people screaming. It sounded great.

As we got closer, I could see the biggest roller coaster in the park, The Tonsil Tamer. It was enormous and towered over the other rides. I also saw the Spider Legs roller coaster.

Just before I got in line, my grandmom said that she wanted to walk up with me to make sure I was buckled into the car. I was humiliated and begged my mom to tell her no. My mom ignored me and I walked up the steep stairs with my grandmom and we waited in line.

It took twenty minutes to get to the front of the line and I stood in the spot for the first car. In a few seconds, the roller coaster came howling into the station and the riders got off. Everyone in line got on and the roller coaster pulled out of the station, clicking its way up the first big hill.

Unfortunately, I was still standing in line. I don't know why, but my feet seemed to be glued to the concrete floor. When the next one pulled in, everyone got off, new people got on, and it left the station. Sadly, I was still standing there and the people behind me started to yell.

As the next train pulled in, my grandmother waited for the people to get off and pushed me through to the other side, toward the exit. I was furious with myself and disappointed that after all the talk, I was too terrified to get on.

Just as I reached the exit, I heard a familiar voice yell, "Hey, look at me!" I turned around to find my little, old grandmother, buckled into the roller coaster, waving with both hands! The roller coaster took off, with my grandmom in the front seat!

The End

Next Stop:

Publishing Your Work

Whether your story is being published in the Washington Post or gently hung on the refrigerator, you are now an author (even though most kids seem to think that you must have an actual book, with your name on the cover, to be an author).

Let's go over the difference. Ready? All writers are authors. Authors that get paid, despite how very little we often get paid, are professional authors. That's the only difference and trust me, sometimes there isn't a very big difference between getting paid and not getting paid!

The great thing about writing is that anyone can do it. Even my five year old daughter, Jessica, and my four-year old son, Patrick, are writers. They just think of stories and I write their words on paper for them.

When you finish writing your story, you definitely have some decisions to make. Answering these questions will help you to decide what your next step will be. So turn the page and get ready to answer!

Would you like to keep the work to yourself?

If the answer is yes, that is fine and wonderful. There is no law, at least that I'm aware of, that says you must share your work with the world. Of course, you may need to share with your teacher, but most teachers will respect your wishes not to share with the class. Keep your work in a private binder or folder, but whatever you do, never throw it away!

Would you like to share your work with some family or friends?

It is a great feeling when you share a story you have worked really hard on and people laugh, smile, or cry as they read it. Knowing that someone gets what you are saying is a tremendous feeling. You can share your story or print additional copies for special people. Stories you have written make wonderful gifts that will be treasured forever.

Would you like to share your work with a larger audience?

If you are a writer who would like to see his/her writing published in a magazine, a great place to start, or eventually a book, there are some things you need to know and some great resources available.

I strongly believe that kids should have their work published, but at the same time, I believe that they should learn how to accomplish this task. The following pages will provide you with some tips and resources that you will find helpful on the road to having your work published in a book or magazine.

Common Mistakes By Aspiring Authors

+ **Not doing your homework**

Having your work published is a major accomplishment and you have to take some time to figure out how publishing works. There are rules that must be followed and editors/publishers have certain expectations. Before you start sending your story to editors, find out what they publish, who reads their magazines or books, and what type of work they publish.

+ **Not matching your work**

If you are a boy and you have written a great story about fly fishing, a good match might be **Boys Life** or **Field and Stream, Jr.** No matter how great the story is, odds are, if you send it to **American Girl**, they will not publish it. By the same token, if a girl writes a poem about her favorite doll, **Boys Life** would not be a good match.

+ **Not reading the magazine or publisher's list**

The best way to find out if your work matches a publisher's needs is to read the magazine or look at their list of books that they have published. This is the best way to get an idea of their tastes.

+ **Not including a great cover letter**

Kids often ask me what a cover letter is and basically, it is the letter you send with your story that tells the publish who you are and why the story will interest him/her. The letter should be brief (short) and describe your story in a way that makes the editor want to read it. If the story is great, but the letter is horrible, chances are that the editor will never read the story.

◆ Not following directions

While it sounds simple, you would be amazed at how many kids do not read or follow a publisher's directions, usually called submission guidelines (what you are sending is called your submission and the guidelines are the rules for it). If the guidelines say 500-700 words, do not think you will get extra credit for sending a 2,000 word story. They will probably throw it away.

◆ Not sending a neat submission

When you send your work, it should be neat, clean, and wrinkle-free. Do not send work that looks like it was in the bottom of your locker or is spotted with tomato sauce. The editor probably doesn't care about what you had for dinner on the night you wrote your story.

◆ Not being patient

Some adult authors spend years, that's right, years, waiting for a publisher to publish their work. You may be lucky and have something published quickly, but it usually takes time. Just be sure that you keep writing new material and sending out submissions while you're waiting for an answer. The worst thing you can do is let time or rejection letters make you quit. If you truly want to be published, never ever give up.

Things You Can Do

- **Read everyday**

Believe it or not, most authors believe that the best preparation for writing is reading as much and as many different kinds of books as you can.

- **Write everyday**

Even if it's a few sentences on the days you don't have time, try to make writing a part of your life. The best way to become a great writer is to write everyday.

- **Use the internet**

With a parent, use the internet to locate contests and writing opportunities for kids your age.

- **Find the Market Guide for Young Writers**

This book, written by Kathy Henderson, provides authors, ages 8-18 with excellent advice and many opportunities to submit your work. Whenever I visit schools I leave the name of this book with principals and librarians so they can share the information with students.

- **Send your work to Franklin Mason Press**

Franklin Mason Press is the only publisher to publish children's work, ages 6-9, in every picture book. The editors will soon be accepting work from children 9-12, so check www.franklinmasonpress.com for updates.

- **Accept criticism**

Sometimes this is very hard, but if someone offers you an honest opinion, at least listen to what he/she has to say. Perhaps his/her eyes are seeing something you have over-looked. Never be afraid to change a story, even after you have finished.

- **Find or start a writing group**

You would be surprised how many writing groups may be in your school, local library, or town. If you can't find any for kids your age, talk to your parents or school librarian about starting one. It's great to have a group with whom to share your stories and writing experience.

- **Enjoy writing**

Whenever you write, whether it's for you or for the world, enjoy every moment of it. Enjoy the struggles, the challenges, and the accomplishment when you complete your work.

Writing Worksheets

Feel free to use or copy the following worksheets to help you pre-write a great story.

Word Web

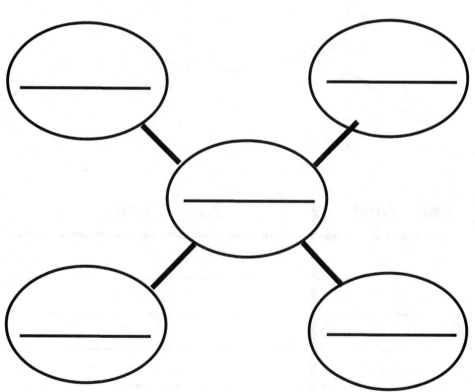

Better Word Web & List

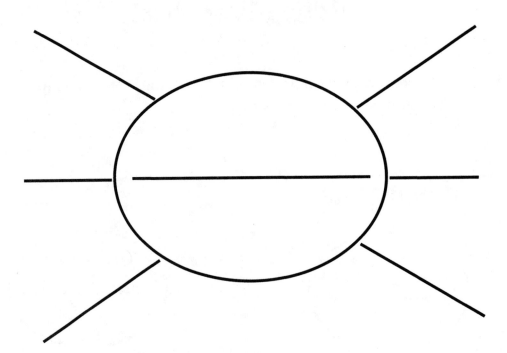

Old Word	New Words

Straight Arrow Map
with a Twist

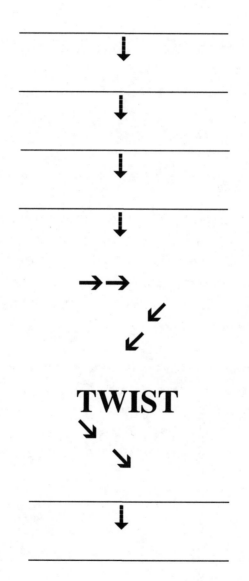

TWIST

About The Author

Lisa Funari Willever is a lifelong New Jersey resident and a former teacher in the Trenton, New Jersey Schools. She is a graduate of The College of New Jersey (formerly Trenton State College) and is married to Trenton Firefighter, Todd Willever. They reside in Mansfield with their children, Jessica, age 5, and Patrick, age 4.

Lisa's dream of becoming an author began at the age of eight years old and she has written 12 books for children, young adults, and teachers, including Everybody Moos At Cows, Chumpkin, 32 Dandelion Court, Where Do Snowmen Go, You Can't Walk A Fish, The Easter Chicken, On YOur Mark, Get Set, Teach, Maximilian The Great, and Exciting Writing: A Handbook For Kids.

Each year, between September and June, she visits 60-70 schools, nationwide, providing School Author Visits and Writing Workshops.

For more information, visit:
www.franklinmasonpress.com